AF230102

Forty Years Later
Life after Alcatraz

by

Alvin Busby

authorHOUSE™

1663 LIBERTY DRIVE, SUITE 200
BLOOMINGTON, INDIANA 47403
(800) 839-8640
WWW.AUTHORHOUSE.COM

First published by AuthorHouse 05/23/05

ISBN: 1-4208-5216-7 (sc)

Library of Congress Control Number: 2005903779

Printed in the United States of America
Bloomington, Indiana

This book is printed on acid-free paper.

This book is for you,
whoever you are,
with deep appreciation---for
without you, the writer part of
me would not exist. . . .

ESCAPE NO. 13
11 June 1962, Monday

	Name: *Clarence Anglin* **Age: 31** **Inmate #:** 1485-AZ **Crime:** bank robbery in Columbia, Alabama **Sentence:** 17 years **Notes:** member of the Anglin brothers robbing team (Alfred, Clarence and John); wanted in Florida for escaping from the Florida State Penitentiary; transferred from Leavenworth after attempting to escape; had also served time in the Atlanta Federal Penitentiary. Status unknown, assumed drowned.
	Name: *John William Anglin* **Age:** 32 **Inmate #:** 1476-AZ **Crime:** bank robbery in Columbia, Alabama **Sentence:** 10 years **Notes:** member of the Anglin brothers robbing team (Alfred, Clarence and John); transferred from Leavenworth after assisting his brother, Clarence, to escape; had also served time in the Atlanta Federal Penitentiary. Status unknown, assumed drowned.

	Name: *Frank Lee Morris*
	Age: 35 **Inmate #:** 1441-AZ **Crime:** bank burglary in Slidell, Louisiana **Sentence:** 14 years **Notes:** wanted for escaping from the Louisiana State Penitentiary while serving time for armed robbery; transferred from Atlanta Federal Penitentiary in January 1961; had an IQ of 133 and was considered the mastermind of this escape. Status unknown, assumed drowned.

At 9:30, Monday night, convicts Frank Morris and brothers John and Clarence Anglin were counted in the last head count of the night. The lights were subdued and the guard in the gun gallery retired for the evening.

The three convicts then placed life-life dummy heads, made from plaster and real hair, and pillows imitating their bodies into their cots. Then they crawled through the mesh-covered air vents in the back of their cells. They had managed to widen the opening of the vents by using mess-hall spoons and knives to chip away the concrete. To conceal their presumably months-long effort, they had created fake vent covers from painted plasterboard which were hidden by accordion cases (Morris) or towels (Anglins).

The three then climbed from their cells, which were located at the bottom tier of B-block, thirty feet up the pipes in the utility corridor behind the cell-block to a ventilator opening at the top. By this evening, they had already removed the rivets from the ventilator cover using a home-made drill converted from an electric fan, and managed to bend the 12-inch crossbar using a crowbar. Taking along life-preservers and an inflatable raft made from raincoats, plywood paddles, and personal effects, they "popped" the cover off the ventilator shaft.

The convicts then climbed onto the roof, and made their way over to a kitchen exhaust pipe at the north end of the roof without being detected by the guard in the No. 1 gun tower. They climbed down the illuminated 50-foot pipe, made their way over two 12-foot barbed fire fences, walked down the pathway near the watertower, across a narrow road, and into a small lumber yard at the edge of the water on the northeastern tip of the island. They put on their home-made life preservers, inflated their home-made raft and went into the water. Then they disappeared forever.

The next morning, Tuesday, at 7:30, the routine morning head-count was started. Morris and the Anglin brothers were not in front of their cells. The guards went in to rouse them and discovered the dummy heads. The alarm was sounded.

A search was made of the entire island. Another convict, Allen Clayton West, was discovered to have also made an enlarged opening covered by a fake cover. When questioned, he stated that he had made his vent too small and, when the others wouldn't wait, was left behind. He also said the plan was to swim to Angel Island using life preservers and an inflatable raft made from raincoats. Angel Island was thoroughly searched, and only a plywood paddle was found.

The Friday after the escape, a waterproof packet was picked up in the bay by a routine debris cleanup by the Army Engineers' Corps. The packet contained photos and addresses that belonged to one of the Anglin brothers. The next day a life preserver, made in the same fashion as those used, was found at Cronkhite Beach, 3 3/4 miles west of the Golden Gate Bridge. Morris and the Anglins are officially listed as missing and presumed drowned. A few days later a body was found at Cronkhite Beach, 3 3/4 miles west of the Golden Gate Bridge. Dental and medical records conclude that the body was not that of Morris or the Anglin's.

For months following the great escape from Alcatraz Prison by Frank Morris, Clarence and John Anglin, there arose great speculation and awe that something like this could even happen. In the year that followed, there were reported sightings of Morris and the Anglin brothers from all over the United States, Canada, and Mexico, but none of them ever panned out to be anything. People were nervous and scared that the escaped convicts could be walking or living right next to them.

There were fourteen escapes from Alcatraz, all of the prisoners were either returned to the prison or was shot in their escape attempt. Frank Morris, Clarence Anglin, and John William Anglin were never found nor even heard of again after their escape. They are still listed by the FBI as: ***'Missing – Assumed Drowned'***, but to this date no one knows for sure. Frank Morris and the Anglin's have been reported to be from Maine to San Diego and all points in between since their escape, but it always turned out to be a false alarm.

One of the many myths about Alcatraz is that it was impossible to survive a swim from the island to the mainland because of sharks. In fact, there are no "man-eating" sharks in San Francisco Bay, only small bottom-feeding sharks. The main obstacles were the cold temperature (averaging 50-55 degrees Fahrenheit), the strong currents, and the distance to shore (at least 1-1/4 miles). Prior to the Federal institution opening in 1934, a teenage girl swam to the island to prove it was possible. The fitness guru Jack LaLanne once swam to the island pulling a rowboat, and several years ago two 10-year-old children also made the swim.

One can never be too sure nor even fully know. Just as the author has written in this book, this is just one of many possibilities. Could it be that Morris and the Anglin's did manage to make it to land somehow, and that their makeshift raft and life preservers really worked? One can never know or be sure . . . .

* * * ONE * * *

It was cold that first Monday in January, Sergeant Turner had just returned to the Sheriff's substation in Derry, New Mexico, a small town in southern Sierra County. Sara, the combination dispatcher and receptionist was at her desk in the front office, she had a look on her face that said she was scared. As he entered he took everything in, just large enough for three offices, a holding cell, interview room, a large front office, and a couple of combination locker room restrooms, it was roughly the size of a four bedroom house, the only exception was that this was a converted double wide trailer and had bars on all the doors and windows.

"What's the matter Sara?" He took off his heavy coat and hat and hung them to dry on the coat rack inside the front door. "Farmer John in the tank again?" He asked with a grin, because he was the local farmer who got tanked every year on the first Monday of the New Year and loved scaring the hell out of Sara.

"N-N-N-No, there is a fed in your office, and he looks mean as nails, I mean hell."

He looked toward the main office, what a federal agent could want here in Derry, we barely have enough crime and domestic violence to keep the four deputies stationed here on a six month rotation busy. He and Sara were the only permanent fixtures here, unless the county decided to close the station. He looked at Sara, she was lovely with her brushed brown hair, button nose, dimples on the high cheeks. But it were her eyes that said it all, they could stare a hole straight thru you or be soft and sinful as if flirting with you.

He looked back at Sara and said, "Call Frank in unit three and tell him that old man Hacklebee had fallen and broke his leg, but he is fine, and they are taking him to the hospital in T or C." Looking back at her, he continued, "I guess I'll go see what our friend wants."

As he walked into the office, the agent was standing with his back to the door, looking at his collection wall. It consisted of diplomas, three citation awards, and a picture of him, his aunt and uncle when he graduated from the Arrey-Derry Independent High School, and a souvenir glass the he had picked up while on vacation and visited the famous *Alcatraz Prison*. The agent was studying the picture intently, he was of medium build, thinning dark hair, glasses set on the bridge of what looked like a broken nose, and wore a brown battered over coat that went to his knees.

"Please do not touch that," he spoke with semi authority, "that is a special souvenir I picked up from *Alcatraz*."

The agent turned around, taking off his glasses as he turned, he sported a goatee that curled under his chin, his chiseled looks were as hard as granite, he had an air about him that spoke authority and do not mess with me. He was dressed in a dark grey suit, a thin black tie and black round toe shoes. He took his gun belt off, and placed it in the top drawer of my desk.

The agent took some papers out of breast pocket, and with a voice that boomed in the still morning air, "Sergeant Joshua Turner lets see, you have been with the Sierra County Sheriff's office for twenty three years."

He picked a file folder and opened it, "Twenty-five, I retire at the end of the year with a full pension and honors." He glanced up at him over the folder He pretended to read.

He continued, "My name is FBI Special Agent Jack Dobsken up from the El Paso office."

"What, may I ask, does the FBI want in Derry or in Sierra County for that matter?"

"Two months ago you submitted fingerprint file cards with some fingerprints on them, we, the FBI are very curious as to where you obtained them?"

"Tell me who's they are and I will tell you where I got them."

"No, you first." Dobsken looked at me as if to say do not make me force my hand, or you will suffer the penalty.

"I lifted them off of that glass on the shelf behind you." He came from around the desk and moved to the collection wall, He pointed to the glass and said, "You see, back in September, I went to San Francisco with my family and we visited *Alcatraz Prison*. The lady on the tour told me that this glass was the last water glass that prisoner *'Frank Lee Morris'* had drank from before his great escape." The agent gave me a look that said *'Yeah, right.'*

"It was in the cell where *Frank Morris* was, I was impressed by the tour guide and I bought it on impulse. Anyway, after returning, I dusted it, lifted some prints and mailed them in, I was intrigued."

"Guess what," the agent gave me a cold stare as I returned back to my desk and the folder. "Not only were your prints on it, but so was the tour guide's, and those of one *Frank Lee Morris*, are you stonewalling me?"

Josh looked up over the folder, shrugged with his lips and eyes, looked at the glass, then back at the agent, and without missing a beat said "Well, I'll be damned, you mean to tell me that that tour guide at the museum was telling me the truth, and that glass was actually held by Frank Morris" He looked jubilant.

The FBI agent gave him a stern and thoughtful look, then pulled up a chair and sat down and took out his notebook. "Forgive me if I doubt you, but as you may know, news of Frank Morris stirs up old memories by some federal agents. So if you do not mind, would you sit down and tell me the story of the glass and prints you sent. Afterwards I am going to have you swear and sign the statement."

Turner sat down and started to relate to the agent his vacation and how he came into the possession of the glass and the prints. Afterwards Sara typed up the two page report which he signed and dated. The agent folded the report, slipped it into an envelope and bid him and his wife good day and started to depart.

He followed him as far as the front door of the station, and waved as he backed up his car and left, I shrugged and went back into the office. As a second glance he half turned and watched the agent, he then picked up the radio mike and spoke into it, "Base to units 2 and 3. Watch for a four door, beige, LTD, report if he does not go south on I25, do not, repeat do not stop, clear."

He then leaned on the counter to wait for the units to report in. Sara came over leaned against him and put her arms around him, "What's wrong Josh, what did he want."

He sighed, "He wanted some information, and I do not know what is wrong right now, give me a little time." I looked down into the eyes of my wife and continued, "Okay?" and smiled.

Frank Oz tore the traffic citation out of the book and gave it to the driver, and told him to please slow down and to come to a full stop at stop signs. He then returned to his cruiser to finish his report on the incident and traffic stop. Out of the corner of his eye he saw the beige LTD pass, go up the road another quarter of mile and turn left toward the interstate. He picked up his mike, "Unit 3 to base, subject just passed and turned to I25, will follow in a minute, out."

Frank then clicked the seat belt, checked traffic and pulled out to follow the car to make sure it went to the interstate highway and head south. As he made the left turn he saw the car make a right turn onto the highway, south. Frank kept driving over the interstate and watched the car pick up speed and head south toward Las Cruces and Texas. On the other side he picked up his mike, "Unit 3 to base, subject is headed south on I25, out." Frank then turned toward Arrey to finish his afternoon patrol.

Back at the station Josh acknowledged both calls from the patrol unit, and breathed a sigh of relief. He turned back toward his wife of twenty years, smiled and said, "I am going to go back into the office, unless the building is on fire, please do not bother me for a while, thanks."

At that he turned and went into his office as he took a coke from the six pack on her desk and went into his office. Because of shoddy dental work, he could not stand things cold anymore, and he though it tasted better luke cold. Taking the picture from the wall, he sat at his desk and slowly sipped the coke. He sat there staring at the man with rectangular shaped face and beard and said to him, *'who the hell are you?'*

Josh Turner had been with the Sierra County Sheriff's office for almost twenty-five years. He was near retirement and the Officer in charge of the substation in Derry which was on the border of Dona Ana and Sierra Counties in southern New Mexico. Because it was located in both counties, Dona Ana let Sierra County do all the patrols and handle the region, and send them reports every six months.

Several years earlier, Sierra County discovered that it was easier and more cost effective to have substations than to have all the deputies located out of one office, so they opened substations in remote areas of the county, with Derry being one of them. His father had been a deputy and one of the first to be assigned to the remote site. His mother and father was killed in a car accident on their return from a wedding reception in the town of Hatch, the drunk had crossed the yellow line of the curve, knocked their car into a ravine and kept on going.

His aunt and uncle had taken him and his brother in and raised them as their own, but always reminded them who their real parents were, and to never forget them. He only knew bits and pieces of his uncle who had wandered into town some forty years ago, never the full story. All he knew was that he had married his aunt and later purchased close to two hundred acres of farm land and was very successful at it.

Josh Turner pulled up to the front of the Sheriff's substation in Derry. It was cool that mid August morning, as he was getting out of the suburban he noticed his uncle's beat up truck in the lot. Although it never officially closed, there was no one on duty at the substation at night, the phones were transferred to the main office in Truth or Consequences, and if needed, a deputy was called at home. Josh was always the first to arrive at the small office, usually at 7AM.

His Uncle, Frank Tanner was asleep behind the wheel of the old Chevy one ton truck, he went up and very quietly said, "What's the matter Uncle Frank, you and Nancy have a fight or something?" Frank jumped at being talked to so suddenly, and quickly looked around as if he was scared of something.

He slowly rubbed the sleep out of his eyes and replied, "No we didn't, and I just need someone else to talk to beside Nancy."

Opening the door of the truck, Josh said, "well come on in Frank, I think the coffee is ready." He always set it to go off at 6:30.

Frank and Josh entered the substation. Josh turned things on lights, radio, the various machines, but did not transfer the phones. That was reserved for his wife Sara who would be in later. Josh poured him and his uncle a cup of coffee and took them into his office which was located behind and just to the left of Sara's work area, the dispatcher and receptionist's desk. He put one down in front of his Uncle and the other on the blotter on his desk. He then took his gun belt off and placed it in the top drawer, took a sip of the coffee and looked at his uncle who was just nursing the cup.

Josh looked at his uncle who was deep in thought. He stood about six foot four inches tall, slender build, had a shock of brown and white hair that he combed to the sides, but it would revert to its natural state of being brushed to the back. It was his facial features that set him apart from other persons. If it wasn't for the natural curves of the jaw and the high cheek bones, his face would be shaped like a box.

He had wide set and hallowed eyes and a large nose that looked like it might have been broken at one time, and a beard. He was a loving father, a good friend to his neighbors, a wonderful grandfather and a great old man of about seventy-six. After awhile Josh looked at him and said, "What is the matter Unc, what do you need to talk about?"

Frank took another sip of his coffee, looked at his nephew and replied, "Have you ever seen the *Clint Eastwood* movie, *Escape from Alcatraz*?"

"Who hasn't, it is on the air almost ever other month." He gave him a thoughtful look and said, "Why?"

"Well, the other night, I was watching it with the two grandkids, and the youngest one asked if things like that really happened." He rubbed his chin and continued, "It got me to thinking, and I decided to come over here."

Josh looked at him, he had a questionable look on his face, "Ok, what does that have to do with you Unc?"

Frank moved closer to the edge of his chair placed his hands on the top of the desk, interlacing his fingers, looked at them, and without hesitation said, "You see," he paused and looked around the office as if searching for the words, "I am the man he portrayed, I am Frank Lee Morris."

Josh was near the edge of his chair taking a large drink of coffee, when his uncle told him this he almost spit it out, instead he quickly swallowed it and choked in the process. He wiped his chin, stood so fast that he spilled some, looking at his uncle with a look of discouragement and anger replied gruffly, "Unc, how in the hell could you say something like that. You know damn well that you are not Frank Morris. He died in that escape attempt in '62." He just glared at his uncle.

His uncle picked up his coffee cup, looked at his nephew and said, "Well, they do say that confession is good for the soul." After taking another drink, continued, "If you do not mind, I would like to confess mine to you."

Josh refilled their cups with fresh coffee, looked at his uncle, who had moved further back into his chair with his cup. Josh went around the desk, and sat opposite of him, leaned back, gestured toward his uncle and said with a slight grin, "I am all ears Unc, go for it."

With that Frank Tanner started his story . . . .

* * * **TWO** * * *

The waves were coming onto the southeast beach of Angel Island, the man laying in the water slowly raised his head and turned to look at the other man there. They were each coughing and spitting sea water out of their mouths. The sun was coming up in the east giving an eerie glow to the bay, the men sat up and looked to the south at Alcatraz prison, turned to each other and smiled. The men looked liked they had just came out of a washing machine, their hair was matted to their heads, their clothes dingy and covered with seaweed they looked clammy and ghost white pale.

Suddenly the younger one jumped to his feet and started calling out, "John, John where are you John, we made it." He turned around and then looked up and down the beach, then looked at the other man, "Frank, where's my brother John?"

Frank looked at him and replied, "I do not know, all I know is that he slipped off the raft before we did, I just do not know." He sat up shock his head and looked around, "I do know that we need to circle the island and get to the north end." The other man started walking toward the beach, "Clarence, don't go on the beach, if they bring dogs they'll be able to track us, stay in the water."

The other man was Clarence Anglin, the younger of the Anglin brothers, who with Frank Morris broke out of Alcatraz Prison. Now they were on Angel Island north of Alcatraz, but his brother John was nowhere to be seen. He then saw the pouch that he made to put pictures and clippings in, he bent down to pick it up.

Frank saw him and said, "Throw it up on the beach where the water can't get to it and leave it."

"Why? This was mine and John's I want to keep it."

"If we leave it, they will think that we did not make it. So, leave it."

At that Clarence threw the pouch up onto the beach, Frank grabbed a paddle and threw it up on the beach as well. Frank then waded over to where some outcroppings were and carefully placed a chrysanthemum on the rocks. He then walked back to Clarence and said, "A present for the warden. He smiled and continued, "We'll stay in the water and circle the island to the north." He looked at Clarence who was gasping for breath, "Are you ready?" Clarence nodded and he continued, "Then let's go."

The two men stayed in the water and circled the island till they were on the north shore of the island, they could hear the boats and helicopters coming. Frank started looking at the outline of the island, he grabbed Clarence's arm and pointed toward another outcropping of rocks. "When we get there, we go under the water."

The two men got to the outcropping, started breathing long and hard then at the last minute, Frank went under the water swimming under the rocks through sort of a tunnel, Clarence following him. It seemed liked hours and then they emerged into a small chamber inside the island and under the rocks. There were ledges on the sides that a person could sit or lay down on. Each man climbed up on a ledge and sat down, they could hear the searchers and dogs above them combing the island for them.

Clarence looked at Frank, "Say Frank, how did you know that this was here, I mean who told you about it."

Frank was looking up at the small hole in the roof area, "English, the prison librarian told me about it." He looked at Clarence "Apparently he is sort of a historian on San Francisco and the surrounding areas. They will not know that we are here if we stay quiet."

"Now what do we do."

"We'll stay here for about two days, and then we swim to the *Tiburon Peninsula*. From there we go where we want." Frank looked up again and said, "Better get some rest."

"Can't we start a fire, I'm cold."

Frank glared "No! The smoke will go up the hole and they'll get us. Now lie down and get some rest." With that, Frank laid down and fell asleep. Frank woke with a start, he slowly looked around, and listened intently for any kind of a sound, hearing nothing he raised on his side, and he looked over and saw that Clarence was still fast asleep on the ledge across from him. He slid down into the murky water below and went under.

Clarence woke and looked around, it was dark and he could barely make out the ledges, looking up he finally saw the hole that Frank had been talking about. He could almost make out a couple of stars, his eyes slowly adjusted to the dark and he looked around some more, Frank was not one the ledge across from him, he sat bolt upright, he quickly looked all around, but Frank was no where to be seen in the cavern, he started to get nervous. He was just about to call out for Frank when he suddenly emerged out of the water.

"Where the hell were you at, I woke up and you weren't here, I didn't know what to do, where were you."

Frank threw some fish up on the ledge next to him, "Getting us something to eat." He then threw some more on the other ledge and crawled out of the water. "we will have to eat them raw, there are a couple of boats circling the island, I saw them while I was out."

"You went out and left me here by myself, I almost panicked, what's going on."

"No need for both of us to go out there and risk getting caught. Besides, I needed to see what was happening out there without a lot of noise or something to distract me. Use this knife gut the fish, wash it in the water, then eat it, like this" with that Frank gutted his sea bass washed it and started eating the meat.

"We have to eat them raw, can't we start a small fire and cook them?"

"No, there are still people out there. We will leave tomorrow night."

"Where are you going Frank?" Clarence asked, eating the fish.

"I thought that I would go to Houston, I have a sister there that I can stay with for a while." He lied as he ate the fish. He did not want Clarence to know where he was going. "And you, where are you going."

"I thought I would go up the coast to Vancouver."

"You mean Canada?"

"Yea, if I make it they will not send me back unless I get into trouble, and I do not aim to get into any."

"Well I hope you make it."

"How you getting to Houston anyway, walk?"

"No, all the inmates got together and gave me a hundred dollars, I am going to get a one way bus ticket, and you." Frank looked up at him over his fish.

"I have about seventy-five from my working at the prisons that I brought, which ought to get me there or close to it."

Frank threw the remains of the fish into the water, "I am going to go back to sleep, talk to you later." With that, Frank lay back down, the rocks were very uncomfortable. The truth was that Frank was going to go to Slidell, Louisiana and retrieve the half million that he hid before he was caught for robbing the bank there. That is, if it was still there.

The water was cold, he knew that Clarence could not survive another night in the cavern or on the island, they would have to attempt to swim to the peninsula tonight. They ate more raw sea bass then slipped into the cold water to leave the cavern. After swimming through the tunnel they emerged outside the cavern and back in the bay. They could see the lights beckoning to them from the peninsula, Frank judged that it was about a mile maybe two to the shore line. He looked over at Clarence, he was paler and even more clammy looking in the moon light than he looked inside the cave. "We have to swim in that direction so that the tide and currents can carry us back towards the shore." He took another look at the land fall, "are you ready?" Clarence nodded.

The swim was long and hard, they would swim toward the east for a while then float and let the current carry them back west. They repeated this procedure for about two hours or so. They finally made the boat docks and the pier at the peninsula, they clung desperately to the pillars that held up the docks, and the waves that were crashing in battered them against the pilings. The stayed under the pier all the way to the shore, they crossed over a low concrete blockage that kept the waves from eroding the sand away from the docks.

There was a pair of security guards walking the pier, they hid behind an overturned row boat till they were out of sight and at the end of the pier, then they made for the street beyond. When they made the street, looked both ways and saw a bus stop with a bench, they crossed the street and sat down on the bench to rest for a while before moving on.

Clarence looked over at Frank, he had his head down between his legs breathing hard and heavy. He coughed a couple of times and then spit onto the street, he then stretched back and leaned on the back of the bench and stretched his legs fully out.

They both looked at each other, the water had soaked their clothes, hair, shoes and socks. It was Clarence that broke the silence, "Well, we are almost totally free."

Frank looked down at his shirt, and then up at the street light, "Yea, we need to ditch these clothes, or find some long overcoats to hide them." He looked over at Clarence who looked like he had just crawled out of a sewer, "If the police see us they will know that we are escapees, lets get moving."

They started walking down the street, a street sign said Beach Boulevard, they keep walking towards the east, and a bank clock said 1:15. The street ended at Tiburon, they turned to the south and kept walking. Frank was constantly looking here and there noticing everything and seeing nothing. Suddenly he stopped, he grabbed Clarence's arm, he looked again, turned to Clarence and told him to stay there, and he would be right back. Frank started across the street and Clarence went behind some trees.

Frank entered the alley behind the Salvation Army building, he did not really know what he was looking for. He rummaged through a couple of cardboard boxes of clothes that people had had left there, he came up with a couple of flannel shirts, some stocking caps, and two long army overcoats that would help warm them up. He emerged from the alley looked both ways and started to cross the street when he noticed the police cruiser coming up the road. He darted back into the alley and covered himself with the clothes, the police car stopped and blocked the alley, and the police officers got out and went into the alley.

Clarence saw the police car about the same time that Frank did, he moved back further into the underbrush and crouched further down trying to hide even more. The police went into alley where Frank was. The flashlights of the police cast eerie shadows on the walls and clothes. "What a mess, I wish these people would clean this up, it attracts bums and thieves."

The second officer kicked at a pile here and pile there, he stopped just short of where Frank was lying and turned to the other, "Yeah but there is nothing we do except keep writing it up, and maybe somebody will do something."

Looking at his watch the other said, "It's late, let's go get a cup of coffee or something."

The officers turned off their lights turned and went back to the police car, they left never really looking or searching for anything. Frank crawled out from under the clothes went to the entrance of the alley, and hurriedly crossed the street. He found Clarence curled up under a bush near a tree, he was shivering from the cold. "Here, I got us some shirts and overcoats, they will help us get warm."

They quickly took off their shirts and put on the flannel ones that Frank had found, then the caps and the coats. They wadded theirs up and stuffed them under the bush and went back to the street. Clarence looked at Frank and gave a sheepish smile, "I feel a little better and a little warmer now, thanks Frank."

"Lets go, I think the bus station is this way."

They walked on for a few more hours, stopping to rest here and there at the various benches at bus stops. From out of nowhere a police car came up behind them and put its lights on. The pair stopped and just stared at the police car, they thought 'great we have just been caught and we are going back to jail.'

The police officer got out of the car and came around the front of the car, he slowly looked the pair up and down. They looked like a couple of bums who were up to no good, and probably looking for a place a rob. "Where are you two going, and what are you doing out here at this time of night?"

Frank quickly spoke up, "We're sorry officer, but we are lost, we came over from San Francisco by bus then went for a walk, and we can't seem to find the bus station." He paused and watched the reaction of the policeman, "If you could direct us to the station we will gladly get a couple of tickets and leave, we do not want to cause any trouble."

The officer shined his light into their faces and up and down their clothes, 'yeah right, it looks more like you just crawled out of pool of water.' He then motioned toward the cruiser, "The station is on the other side of town." He opened the back door, "You two get in and I will take you there, and watch as you get your tickets." He closed the door and walked back to the driver's side, he looked in the back again, 'there is something very familiar about those two, and I just can't put my finger on it.' He started the car and made a right turn.

Ten minutes later the car pulled up into the lot of the Greyhound bus terminal, the officer got out and opened the back door and motioned the pair out. "All right, let's go inside and get your tickets." He followed the pair into the terminal, as soon as they could not or would not get tickets he would bust them and take them in.

The terminal was quiet this early in the morning, most of the shops were closed and only two tellers were there. The pair went to the first empty window, they were a little nervous with the policeman directly behind them. Clarence looked at the woman behind the counter, she was pretty, long blonde hair, dark eyebrows. She looked at Clarence and said, "Can I help you." She never gave him a second glance.

"I want a one way ticket to *Blaine, Washington* please." The woman did some entrees on the terminal.

"How many."

"One" Clarence replied and took his money out of his pants pocket.

The woman did some more entries looked at Clarence and replied, "That will be sixty seven fifty. Board at gate number three that says Portland." She counted out his change and gave him his ticket booklet.

"Next," the woman looked at Frank and gave a sour look. Frank's left eye was all red, and blood soaked from scraping the rocks in the tunnel. "Where are you going?"

Frank looked at her as if to say 'screw you bitch', "I want a one way to Slidell, Louisiana."

The woman did entries on the terminal, asked Frank the same questions she did Clarence, she came back, "That will be eighty nine ninety."

Frank gave her the money and waited for his change and ticket book. As she gave it to him she said, "Board at gate number five that says Los Angeles." She gave Frank his ticket book and change and turned and walked away from the window, she thought she was going to be sick.

Frank pocketed his ticket and change, turned and walked to the bathroom to wash his hands and face. The police officer stopped him and asked where he was going, Frank looked at him coldly, and he had the beginnings of a headache. "To the bathroom." The officer stepped aside and watched him then turned his attention to Clarence.

Frank walked out of the bathroom fully expecting to see a barrage of police and men with guns drawn to take them back to prison, instead he saw the officer with a bag in his hand. "I will make you the same offer I made the other guy." He held it out waiting for a reply.

"What's the offer?"

"Here is bag with a loaf of bread, bologna, and a cup of coffee, it's yours for five bucks."

Frank was taken aback, he never thought that the officer would do that, he looked at him, smiled and counted out the five and gave it to him. The officer put it in his pocket then said, "Now, I am going to stay here till both of you get on your chariots and leave, you try to run and I will shoot you down." With that, Frank took the bag and sat down in one of the chairs, took out the coffee and began to drink, it tasted good.

At six the speakers in the terminal came to life and announced the departure of Clarence's Bus to Portland, Seattle, and other points north, and that all persons with tickets were to board the bus at gate number three. Frank got up with Clarence and walked with him to the door. Clarence turned and looked at Frank.

He reached out his hand and Frank took it, "We made it." There were tears of joy coming out of his eyes.

Frank grinned gave a sideways look, "Yea, you just listen to the driver's instructions and you will make it." After a pause he turned back to him, "You take care and stay out of trouble."

"Thanks Frank." Clarence turned and went through the door to the bus, gave his ticket to the driver, turned and waved then boarded the bus, went toward the back and sat down.

Thirty minutes later the speakers came to life again and announced Frank's bus and destinations. He started walking to the door, the police officer grabbed his arm and Frank froze in his tracks. He slowly turned and looked at the policeman solemnly, "Yes sir."

"Just wanted to say thanks to you and your buddy. I guess you two were telling the truth, we get all kinds of bums coming over here from Frisco, and we just do not trust them." The officer stuck out his hand, and Frank took it in earnest and shook it twice, and the policeman continued, "Buddy, just do me a favor, when you get where you are going, take a bath, okay?"

Frank looked at him and smiled, "I sure will, and thanks for the bread and stuff." He then turned and boarded the bus, he went all the way to the back of the bus and sat down. He was still a little nervous, and would be until the bus left California.

The officer stayed in the terminal until both buses backed up and left the terminal. He still had this funny felling that he had seen both men before somewhere. He passed a paper machine, almost bought a paper, and then decided against it. On the back side of the paper on the bottom of the front page were pictures of the three convicts who had recently escaped from Alcatraz. Had the officer bought one, he would have immediately recognized them, but he didn't so it bothered him for several years.

The officer went out to his cruiser and checked in. He straightened up the fliers that he had in the front seat, one was of three escaped convicts, but the pictures were so bad that he could not see them clear enough to make a positive identification, even if he did see them. Besides, the news conference that had been held at the prison said that the three had probably drowned in the bay, because all the evidence that they had found indicated this.

The bus with Frank Morris on it went across the bay on highway 580 into Richmond then went west into Nevada. He was on his way to Slidell and hopefully his half million dollars. Frank opened the bag and made several dry sandwiches and devoured them. He wiped his mouth then settled back and fell fast asleep.

* * * THREE * * *

The bus finally arrived at Slidell at four in the afternoon on Sunday. The terminal was not very busy, but it was crowed, it was the local hang out for most of the bums and low life in Slidell. Frank walked out the front door and orientated himself with where he was at. His beard had grown more over the past two days to where it would be hard for anyone to recognize who he really was.

The bus terminal was located at the corner of Front Street and Fremaux Avenue, the church was on Florida somewhere near Michigan. So he started walking that way to see what was in store for him and how easy it would be. On the way he pasted a K-Mart with a motel across the street from it. He stopped and looked these over, if the money was still there, he would come back and get a room then some new clothes.

He watched the people walking up and down the streets and the cars driving by, none of them were particularly watching him or even noticing him. It was he who was watching them, he wanted to get this over with and then leave. To where he had no idea, but he wanted to be anywhere but here. When he reached Michigan he turned right to walk down to the church.

As he was approaching the church, he happened to pass the branch of the Slidell National Bank that he had robbed that cold winter day in 1961. There was a faded sign in the front window that read: *'We were robbed by Frank Lee Morris, Who drowned while escaping Alcatraz.'* Frank read the sign and grinned, if they only knew he thought. He continued on down the street constantly looking and watching the people on the street. Then suddenly he was in front of the Catholic Church where he had hid the money. He stood in front of it and examined it in awe.

He never had the time back then to take in the wonder of the church, he was on the run looking for a place to hide the money. The front of the church was impressive with the carved pillars that looked like they held up the front of the over hang of the front. Then there were the stained windows on either side of the doors and the ones in the door itself. He never noticed the cross over the door before, most of the time when he viewed crosses they had the body of *Christ* on them, for some reason this one did not. He was looking so intently that he failed to hear or even notice the police car pull up behind him.

The police officer came up behind him and said "Excuse me sir do you need some help?"

Frank turned and looked at the officer, he looked to be about twenty five, had a triangular shaped face, small nose, close set eyes, brown curly hair under his blue police hat. He was dress entirely in blue with a white stripe down the outside edge of his trousers. His right hand rested on his gun that he had unstrapped, he was intently looking Frank up and down. "I asked you mister, do you need some help." He was as nervous as Frank was.

"N-no I do not officer, I am just passing through, and I stopped to admire the front of the church here." Frank semi lied to the policeman.

"Well, I have been watching you since you came out of the bus terminal, what are you doing here."

"I came down from Colorado to visit my sister, but when I called her from the station I found out that her and her family is out of town. So, I thought that I would walk around some."

"You need to find a place and get off the streets."

Frank looked at him and frowned, "May I ask why, I mean I just got into town."

"This is University bash week-end and we are expecting problems and if you are on the street and a stranger, you will be picked up and arrested."

Frank looked at him, nodded half turned towards the Church and replied, "Does that mean that I cannot go in and pray?"

"That is correct, you need to move on now or I will take you in."

Before Frank could answer, the doors of the Church opened and a priest dressed in black with a white collar under his neck emerged. The priest had hardened looks, sported a full beard, and wore black horn rimmed glasses with a chain on the ear pieces that went around the back of his neck. "Good evening gentlemen, is there some kind of problem here."

Frank quickly said, "Father Flanner? Is that you, it is Frank Tanner, the boy you helped out several years ago." He shot a quick glance toward the policeman and continued. "I was wondering if you could help him out again."

The priest looked at him, squinted his eyes trying to recognize him. "No, I am Father Walker, Father Flanner has not been here for quiet some time, but I am sure that he would want me to continue with his work." He stood to one side his back to the door that was ajar and beckoned toward the inside of the Church, "Please come inside, unless the officer has an objection."

The policeman started to back up and look down at the ground, and then back up, he looked at Frank, then the Priest, then back to his patrol car. "No Father, I have no objection." He looked around again, "Its just that I do not want him to be on the streets tonight."

Father Walker looked at the policeman sternly "Do not worry he will spend the night then leave in the morning." He looked at Frank and gestured with his head toward the open door. "He will leave in the morning after he is well rested." He then looked at the Policeman, "John, I want to see you in church much more often."

The policeman nodded, waved jumped into his cruiser, thankful to be gone from there.

Frank went up the wide steps and into the Church. It had been a long time since he had been inside a

Catholic Church. His parents were strict and devoted Catholics, maybe that was why he turned bad, guess he rebelled against them. He took in the whole awe of the inside of the church, the high vaulted ceiling, the way that they blended in with the beams that made up the walls. Then he saw the little niche next to the third confessional, the loose bricks after all this time was still there though not very visible, but they were still there.

The priest looked at Frank as he led the way, "Did you really know Father Flanner, or was that a ruse to get inside the church."

"No, I really knew Father Flan as we called him." He looked at the bricks one last time. "I grew up around here, I was a rebel and Father Flan tried his best to change me."

"I heard that Father Flanner took in some of the boys and tried to help them." He turned the corner and gestured down a long hall. "The kitchen is this way. I was on my way to evening prayers when I saw you outside, then saw the officer drive up, guess I saved you just in time." He smiled and his teeth looked yellow from tobacco stains.

He led him into the kitchen and started to get stuff out to feed him. "I hope that eggs and bacon is fine, it is about all that the food bank brings me any more." After a pause he continued, "After you eat I will show you to a room with a bath where you can clean up, and I will get you some fresh clothes after I finish my prayers."

After the blessing they ate in silence, neither one said anything, for that was the way at the dinner table in the church. You did not talk, you simply ate. After wards the priest did the dishes and Frank helped by drying. The priest rambled about things of non importance. Frank did not pay attention, he too busy thinking about the bricks in the wall. He had to hurry for it was getting dark outside, and he could not afford to turn on the lights.

The priest then showed him down the hall to a room, the priest looked him up and down and side to side. "Wait right here and I will be right back." The priest left, then quickly returned he laid some things on the small cot bed. "Here are some pants, a shirt, socks, underclothes and two towels and some soap." He pointed toward the back of the room, "There is a small bathroom you may clean up and change into these. Now, I am off for prayers."

The priest left and Frank watched him. He went into another room further down the hall, closed and locked the door. Frank turned and quickly looked around the room, it was plain and simple, a small cot bed, a combination dresser and writing table. In the top drawer was a flashlight. He tried it and it worked. He then quietly opened the door and slipped out.

He made his way back down the hall, through the kitchen, into the other hall and finally into the church. It was still barely light enough for him to make his way across the room passed the benches in the church to the other side. He got on his knees and pried at the bricks, they were a little hard to pull out, but they finally came. Reaching into the hole he scraped his arm on the other bricks and felt around. He reached in even further and finally felt the bag, he grabbed a handle and drugged it out. It was a small green army looking supply bag with a zippered opening, very carefully he unzipped it and shined the light inside. There sitting on top of the money was the gun that he had used.

He picked up the gun turned it over and over, slowly looking at it. He decided he did not need it and shoved it back into the hole, he then pushed the bricks back into place, zipped up the bag and went back to his room.

Frank was lying on the cot thinking what to do next, he could not help but think of Clarence, what was he doing, did he make it, are the bills in the bag traceable? Sometimes he wished that he smoked so that he had something else to do besides just thinking thoughts. Frank was unaware that all banks did record serial numbers of large bills, the bank that he had robbed several years ago did not record any of the bills that he had gotten. That night he had a restless sleep, tossing and turning, waking looking and going back to sleep.

There was a light rap on the door to his room and he sat up quickly. He looked around to orientate himself to where he was. Then from the other side came the priest's voice, "Mister Tanner are you awake?"

Frank looked at the door, "Yes I am."

"Good as soon as you are dressed come to the kitchen for breakfast, all right?"

"Yes Father as soon as I get dressed."

Frank came walking into the kitchen carrying his old clothes in one hand, in the other was the green bag and over coat in the other. "What should I do with these?"

The priest looked up "Just put them in the garbage there in the corner. You may either keep those clothes or bring them back from your sister's. How do you feel?"

"I feel much better after the shower and change of clothes, thank you."

The priest fixed the breakfast while Frank sat the table, he glanced at the clock, seven am. They ate in silence, questions going through each of their minds. They finished their breakfast, cleaned up the kitchen, then sat and drank coffee, the priest lit up a cigarette, he looked at it, "bad habit I picked up, I only do it two or three times a day."

Frank looked at him, grunted and nodded, "never tried, was always tempted, but never did."

"That's good." He paused looked deep into Frank's eyes, "what are you going to do and go."

"I do not know right now, I may drift around a bit." Frank looked back at the priest with a cold nonchalant stare.

"Let me give you some advice," the priest looked at his watch stubbed out his cigarette and continued, "Find a small town somewhere, get a place to live and a small job that way the authorities may leave you alone, and you will not have to seek refuge like this." He smiled, raised his eyebrows, looked around the kitchen and waved at the surroundings.

As if an after thought he said, "I have to get ready for church, there is a small following during the week, but I am obliged to give a sermon seven days a week." He stood, stuck out his hand which Frank accepted, "Good luck to you my son."

Frank nodded and said his goodbyes and left. As he was leaving he took one last look around, took some bills out of the bag and dropped them into the collection plate that was on the table near the door. The priest was at the door greeting people as they came in, he again said goodbye to Frank as he left, he watched him go and said to himself as he noticed the bills, *'Thank you mister Morris, may God go with you in your travels.'* For he knew who Frank was from the minute he entered the church. He and Frank had grown up together in Slidell, even though Frank did not recognize him, he recognized him.

Frank gave the church one finale look, and then started to retrace his steps that brought him here the day before. At long last he was standing in front of the K-Mart he had seen the day before, he looked and noticed that it would not open for a few hours. He turned and noticed the cop that had he had encountered last night, he smiled to himself and thought, *'as long as I do not break any laws, he cannot touch me.'* He walked to the corner, waited for the light and crossed the street, he went to the motel and obtained a room, he would wait there till the store opened.

Frank was pushing the cart down the men's aisle looking for some blue jeans when he spotted the coveralls. He liked the look of them and decided to purchase these instead of the blue jeans that required a belt. He found a large back style bag with one shoulder strap that he could keep his things in, then got some small food items and after looking things over figured he had enough. As he was leaving after making his purchase he asked the store manager if he could take the stuff across the street in the basket and then return it later, the manager gave his blessings.

After cleaning up and washing all the clothes, Frank returned the cart to the K-Mart store then walked down to a restaurant to get something to eat. On the way he stopped at the bus terminal and bought a one way ticket for the next day to Santa Fe, New Mexico. After leaving the restaurant, his belly full he ran into the police officer he met in front of the church. "I have been watching you all day, and I am curious where you got the money?"

Frank gave him a sour look, "my sister came by the church last night and gave it to me. She also told me that her husband did not want any thing to do with me so in the morning I am going to get on the bus and go to New Mexico for awhile." He gave a side glance to the restaurant, "Any objections officer." he said it in a sarcastic tone.

The officer took a step backwards, "No, I am just glad that you are leaving, I personally do not like you, and I will watch and make sure that you do." The police man was just as sarcastic and just a little more irritated.

After returning to the motel Frank packed the bag with what he would not need in the morning then stretched out on the bed and watched the television, especially the news. There was nothing on it about the escape or anything else that mattered except the increased tense situation in Southeast Asia. In the morning Frank left and boarded the bus bound for west Texas and New Mexico, as was his word the policeman was there watching.

From Dallas to El Paso Frank struck up small conservation with the Driver, he confide to the driver that he was looking for a small town somewhere that he could semi disappear into. The driver gave him a long stare through his mirror, grunted shifted gears and kept on driving. The driver noticed that Frank would not eat in the restaurants along the way, but rather would get a loaf of bread some bologna, cheese and cokes and ate dry sandwiches along the way.

After navigating through two accidents and a long detour the bus finally arrived in El Paso, as they were approaching the terminal, the driver was thanking everybody for riding with him and explaining how to get to the various transfer buses that would take them on to their next destination. The Driver watched as Frank got off the bus and went into the terminal and sat down in one of the chairs across from the gate that he would board at.

The driver came into the terminal and went behind the counter and was taking care of the usual business, talking about the trip in, what was wrong with the bus, how long a drive it was, all the while, watching Frank. After he was finished he leaned against the counter, propped his foot on a box, and rubbed his chin and looked at Frank.

The teller brought him a soda, he thanked her, lit a cigarette and walked toward Frank, and he sat in the empty chair next to him. Frank gave him a curious look, but did not say anything, just looked at the clock. After taking a drink the driver said, "You know there are two small towns north of here that might interest you," he gave Frank a quick look, "the first one is Derry and the other one is Arrey." He finished the drink and cigarette and continued.

"Now, I know the Deputy Sheriff in Derry. If you mention my name, he may help you out."

Frank looked at him from the side of his eyes, "Help me where? Into jail."

The driver gave a snorted laugh, "No, he could help you find a place to stay and maybe a job. The driver straightened up in the chair and turned toward Frank, "I know when people are on the run, but you look like a good egg so I am trying to help you out here." He gave Frank a tern look then turned away.

Frank looked at him hard, then hung his head, "Listen mister, I am sorry its just that half of the time I do not know if people are trying to help me or themselves, forgive me."

The driver shrugged his shoulders, smiled and said "Forget it." He looked at the clock and continued,

"When you get to Derry, tell the sheriff that his brother sent you, and he will help you get settled."

Frank was taken aback when the driver told him this. He started to say something but the words would not come, the driver just sat there and stared blankly forward. After awhile the driver broke the silence by standing and turning toward Frank said, "Tell Deputy Jim Grady that his brother Christopher sent you and you will not have any problems." The driver stuck his hand and Frank took it. "I have to go get some sleep, I have to drive back to Dallas, you take care."

Frank could not believe his ears, he just stared as the driver went back behind the ticket counter and disappeared into the driver's lounge. He sat there and stared at the boarding door, *'could it be that he would be able to find a place and disappear?'* The speakers in the terminal came to life and announced the departure of Frank's bus at gate number three, Las Cruces, Albuquerque, Santa Fe and points north. As he went through the door he looked at the counter one last time, smiled turned and got on the bus.

The driver was taking tickets and asking where people were going, he looked at Frank's ticket, "Going to Santa Fe, huh?"

Frank looked up at him, "No, changed my mind, going to get off in Derry, is that all right?"

The driver frowned, "Your loss of money, but I will announce Derry." He wrote the stop down on his driving orders.

As the bus pulled out of the terminal for the trip north, Christopher came out of the driver's lounge, he had taken off his shirt and tie. He stood there in his t-shirt his belly stick out from under it. He smiled big, this might be the answer he and his brother was looking for. He crossed to the counter to the phones, he quickly made a phone call then went back to the lounge, and he turned and watched the smoke curling up from the departing bus.

* * * **FOUR** * * *

It would normally take a person about three hours to drive from El Paso to Derry, but because of the stops, twists and turns that buses makes it took a little over five. The bus finally came to a stop in downtown Derry, and Frank stepped down off the bus and took a slow look around. The driver yelled at him, "You got any baggage?"

Frank turned and at him through the open door shook his head and replied, "No, I have everything with me."

The driver nodded, "Good bye and good luck."

Frank was standing in front of the Derry Mercantile, advertising food, gas and various other products. He opened the right side of the double screen doors and went inside, there were all types of goods on the shelves, and the man behind the counter was old and grizzled looking and kept an eye on all customers that came through the door. Frank walked around the store looking at what there was, picked up a loaf of bread, bologna, and a small package of cheese and decided to get a large bottle of water.

He went to the front to pay for his stuff and to look at the ads that were posted on the bulletin board. He went back outside and decided to walk north, the same way the bus went when it left, after walking about a half a mile he stopped and sat down on a block that was next to a concrete culvert of one of the many irrigation canals that cut paths across Derry. He was sitting there eating dry sandwiches and drinking his water when the Sheriff's car drove past going south, it suddenly turned around came back and stopped in front of Frank.

The deputy got out and came around the front of the car and stopped in front of Frank. He stood there with his arms folded across his chest, staring down at Frank. He was dressed all in brown with the exception of his boots and hat which were black. He sported a leather looking heavy waist length coat with fur on the collar. He was of medium build, with a leathered face that had seen a lot of sun and wind, his eyes could bore right through you. He place his left hand on his hip and pushed his hat back with his right to reveal a touch of balding dark brown hair. That was when Frank saw the name tag, it said *'Grady'*. The same name as the bus driver from El Paso.

The deputy spoke for the first time, he was gruff and short, "We do not take to vagrants here."

"Your brother Chris sent me here" Frank shot back, just as gruff. He looked him over again and noticed that he did not carry a weapon.

"My brother huh?" He kept staring at him, trying to break him. He had a square jaw with a clef in the chin, small eyebrows, and a pox mark on the left cheek. His forehead wrinkled when he talked showing signs of worry, "where did you meet him?"

"At the terminal in El Paso," pausing, he noticed a state police car pull up. "He drove the bus from Dallas to El Paso, and told me to look you up and you could help me get settled here maybe."

The State police officer slowly came around the back of the sheriff car, his hand nonchalantly on the butt of his gun. Frank had kept one eye on him from the moment he had driven up. "Need any help Jim?" The sheriff deputy stepped half to one side and back, and looked at the state police officer. He was young and looked as if he had just got out of the academy, even though he had been on the force for five years and knew the deputy for two.

"No, I have the situation under control," he looked back at Frank and frowned. "This is a guy my brother sent here."

The sheriff turned and motioned for the state police officer to follow him. They walked back to the state police car, the deputy all the while talking to the other officer, and ever once in a while giving a quick glance at Frank to make sure that he did not leave. They shook hands in front of the cruiser, the state patrolman got into his car and left.

The deputy then returned, open the back door of the cruiser and then motioning to Frank said, "Get in, and let's go."

"Go, go where?" Frank was puzzled. What had they talked about?

"You'll find out, now come on." The deputy sounded upset. So Frank reluctantly got up and got into the patrol car. The ride was short and strewn with potholes, they went north a couple of miles then turned west onto an old farm road that had a couple of twists, then over a rickety bridge that forged the river. Frank turned and looked as they crossed it, and the bridge looked as though it would not stand much more. They continued on the road with fields on each side that were overgrown with weeds they turned to the left and entered a large clearing area. All the while, the deputy hardly spoke except to say that the roads to where they were going were rough and bumpy.

In the clearing was a house with a large shop garage style building on the north side on the south was a large looking barn with a lean-too shed on the north side that ran the entire length of the barn. These buildings were at an angle to the house, the front of all three faced them, and just on the other side of the shop was a small trailer that looked livable. As they drove up three kids came out of the house, followed by what Frank thought was the prettiest woman he had seen in a while. Though she wore no make up, she was a beautiful sight, the children were clinging to her dress and apron.

The deputy got out, opened the back door for Frank to get out. "Stay where I can watch you, I'm going to talk to my sister." He turned and walked towards the woman who was coming down the porch steps one at a time sideways. She wore an ankle length blue cotton dress with white flowers on it, over this she wore a dirty brown apron that went over her head and tied in the back. She held her hand over her eyes and watched as Frank walked around.

Frank looked around the clearing that was the front yard, driveway, work and play area all in one, he noticed the kids watching him as well. The place looked as though a tornado had gone thru, there was lumber, tin, cans, glass and other debris scattered all around. He finally worked his way up to one of the main doors to the garage, he pulled it open to look inside, it got half way open then fell and stuck in the ground open. He found the light switch and went inside.

Jim walked up to his sister and gave her a slight hug, "Hi sis, how is it going?"

"Just fine," she was watching Frank, "who is that? Why did you bring him out here?"

"He's the guy that Chris called me about early this morning." He watched as Frank walked to the garage. "Told me the guy just might be what we are looking for out here and to give him a chance." He watched Frank disappear into the garage, "but I don't know." He started to go that when his sister grabbed his arm and stopped him.

"How about," she paused and Frank emerged from the garage with a shovel, hoe and something in his back pocket, "if we give him a chance since Chris vouched for him?" She looked at her brother almost pleading.

He watched as Frank sat down in a chair and started sharpening the hoe, "Ok, I'll go talk to him, he can stay in the trailer." He gave his sister a peck on the cheek, "see you later Nancy."

He watched as she hobbled up the steps and back into the house, and then walked over to where Frank was now working on the shovel. "Before we get started I want to know your name."

Without looking up Frank said, "Tanner, 'Frank Wilson Tanner'." Frank used his real name, not the one that he had given the police when he was arrested for robbing the bank, he had gotten that one from the guard and teller at the bank. He looked up, "I am not looking for trouble, just a place to stay and live."

"I am going to try you out here for a while. And see how good you are to your word" the sheriff looked at the hoe and the shovel, there had been years of rust and dirt on both and were not sharp, but Frank had cleaned and sharpened them very fine.

"May I ask who I am working for, and what I can and cannot do?"

The deputy gave him another look up and down, and then pulled up another chair that was outside the garage, and took his hat off. "That is my sister, her name is Nancy Carter. Her and her husband was in a car wreck about two years ago." He stopped and looked back towards the house, did not see anyone and continued, "He died and she was injured very badly, and almost lost her right leg."

"Any way, she will not sell or leave the place, and it is hard for her to find good help." She is trying to farm the fifty acres she has left, but is no good at it."

Frank looked toward the house as well, "Fifty? Does that mean she owns more?" He was only curious.

"Had, she had to sell two hundred to pay for the hospital, doctors, and funeral," he paused and looked toward the sky. "The drunk that hit them had no insurance and no driver's license." He looked Frank dead in the eyes, "You are not to tell her any of this, you hear." He pointed a broken finger at him and shook it.

Frank looked at him wide eyed, he had never seen that look from any one before, and nodded that he understood.

"You stay here in the trailer and help her out, I'll check on you at some of the most inconvenient times, so keep your nose clean." He got up retrieved his hat and said, "I'll stop by this evening, bring you some groceries, and check on you. Any questions?"

"Maybe later, but not right now." Frank watched as the deputy turned and started to walk away, and then came back. "Also, those kids may be frightened of you at first, you take extra care of them." At that the deputy got into his cruiser and left.

After a few minutes Frank got up and started cutting down the weeds between the garage and the trailer. He had been at for about two hours without any rest when he heard a noise behind him. He jumped and whirled around and saw her there holding a jug and glass, two of her three kids were behind her.

"I thought maybe you would thirsty, so I brought out some tea."

Frank thanked her and took the glass and drank all that was in it and let her refill it. She was looking at the area that he had cleared of weeds. "That must be extremely hard, we haven't had rain for a few weeks, and it looks a lot better, thank you."

Frank nodded and said, "You're welcome, miss" he let the sentence trail off even though he already knew her name.

"I'm sorry, my name is Nancy, Nancy Carter, this is Robert, and the little shy one is Robin."

Frank knelt, looking at the kids, "It is nice to meet you both, but until I get all the boards out there picked up and the nails removed, please wear shoes."

Robert had dirty blonde hair that fell all around his head as if someone had put a bowl over it and cut the hair. "Aint got none" And ran off. The little girl just stood there peeking around Nancy's dress, not knowing what to do.

Frank stood and reached his hand out, "It is nice to meet you." He looked at the glass in the other hand, "and the tea sure hit the spot, thanks."

Nancy quickly shook his hand then withdrew it and brushed the hair back off her cheek. "If you want, there are water spigots around." She blushed then turned and hobbled away leaving Frank alone with his work, Frank watched her all the way to the house.

Around six Jim pulled up in his cruiser and looked around. He pushed the hat back on his head and gave a low whistle. Frank had cleared all the weeds from around the garage and had picked up over half of the wood and tin that was scattered around the yard. To say the least he was impressed with Frank's first five hours of work. He walked over to where he was leaning against the trailer. "How about if we take the food in and get the power on?"

Frank looked at him and smiled, "Thanks, but I have already done that and cleaned it out as well and thought I would rest a while,"

"You have certainly earned it." Jim looked around the place again, scratched his chin, "After we get the stuff inside, I'll leave and see you in the morning." He stuck his hand out and Frank took it.

* * * FIVE * * *

As the weeks wore on and turned into months the visits from officer Grady became less and less. Then six months later Jim Grady showed up in his own car about seven in the morning, Frank was walking from the trailer to the garage to start the morning chores when he noticed him pull up. As he was getting out Frank stopped and waved, "Morning Jim, what's up."

Jim came walking up to him, noticing that he had gotten another pair of work boots. "Nothing, I came over to ask you some personal questions that have been on my mind for quite some time now."

"Sure, go ahead, I have nothing to hide." Frank was worried that he had been found out and that Jim was here to take him back in, his grip tightened on the hoe he had in hands.

"I need to know why you do not have a driver's license, birth certificate or social security card." Jim kept an eye on Frank to detect any sudden movements. He noticed that he had a death grip on the hoe, and that it loosened up just a little bit.

Frank looked at Jim, he was lost in thought, and he had to come up with a good one for this. He had never been asked as to why he did not have any of these documents before. Jim was dressed in a blue plaid shirt, blue jeans, boots, and had his service revolver around his waist. After a short while he responded, "I never had any of those because I thought that I would never need them."

"What do you mean never needed them." It was more like a question than a statement.

"I was born back in the swamps of Louisiana and my momma and daddy hardly went to town." Frank pulled a couple of chairs over for them to sit in and he continued. "When I was born, it was in the swamp land and it was never legally recorded, so I do not have a birth certificate." He looked toward the main house and saw Robert come running out towards them and he continued. "As far as the driver's license and social security card, I do not know how to drive and I only worked for cash, so I never had them."

Jim looked thoughtfully at Frank, *'do I believe him or not'*. He then noticed that Robert was standing there beside Frank, leaning up against him and noticed that he had on shoes and socks, he hadn't wore them for over a year, ever since Frank arrived he noticed that the kids seemed to be more full of life than ever before, so was his sister.

Frank leaned back in the chair and whispered something in Robert's ear then turned and winked, after which he ran back to the house. Frank turned back to Jim, and was deep in thought, he did not totally lie to

Jim. It was true that his birth was not legally reported, but he was not born in the swamps, his parents were staying at motel in town and he was born there because they could not afford the hospital. As for the other, he knew how to drive but had no license, and the places he had worked required no card.

Jim stood and stretched, "Well, let's go."

"Go," Frank was puzzled. "Go where?"

"To Truth or Consequences so we can get everything you need." Jim started walking towards the car, "In order for you to stay and work here you are going to need them." He opened the door and leaned on the roof, "Besides I know several people where we are going to go, they will be able to get it done in no time, so come on." With that he got in and started the car.

It had taken about four hours to get the documents. The social security card and driver's license was easy, it just some entries onto a computer terminal. Getting the birth certificate was the problem, they had to wait for information to be transmitted, and then returned, questions asked, responses sent, but finally they had one. But, because Jim was a deputy sheriff and vouched for Frank the process went fast and by the back door way.

The drive back to the farm was a short one, neither one talked much except to discuss the weather and the seasons. Then Jim pulled the car over and looked straight at Frank. "Listen, I try not to get involved with my sister's affairs, but she has told me that she likes you very much, and well I do not want to see her hurt." He looked down the road and turned back to Frank,

"You understand where I am coming from?" Frank nodded but did not say anything, he found it hard to believe what Jim had just told him.

While cleaning out the barn a few days later Frank found an old beat up 1958 Chevy pickup and a John Deere tractor, he spent two days dragging and pulling them into the garage and then finally got them to running and working. He could then go to town and look for used equipment to use on the farm, on one of his trips he walked into the Powers Real Estate to talk to the real estate agent, but he was not there so he left a message.

The car came slowly up the drive to the semi circle drive that was in front of the house and the out buildings. Frank had been at the farm now for almost six months and was putting the finale touches on the door of the barn and testing it out. The man got out of the car chewing on a big cigar and looked the place over, he was impressed by what Frank had done to the place, and it was down right nice.

Frank walked over to the man who had gotten out of the car, "Howdy, we don't get many visitors, can I help you."

The man took the cigar out of his mouth stuck out his hand and said, "The name is Hank Powers, I understand that you are looking for me?"

"Yes sir, I am interested in buying back the land that Nancy Carter sold you some years back."

The man started laughing like someone tickled his funny bone, then spat between his boots. Then gave Frank a modest sour look, "You've got to be shitting me mister. Where would you get that kind of money?"

"I don't know, I haven't heard the price yet?"

The man cocked his head to one side, squinted his eyes and said, "Lets see, I figure a hundred fifty thousand should do it." He gave Frank a look that said I dare you. The man was almost as round as he was tall, he had no neck, his head just met his shoulders where one should be. He had hands that were the size of bear paws, and his face was round and fat as well. You could barely make out his eyes through the slits, and his nostrils flared when he talked as if he had problems breathing.

Frank gave him a hard look, and after a while spoke soft and low, "I'll see what I can do."

The fat man gave him a business card with a hatch, NM address and said, "When you are ready, come see me." With that the man turned got back into his car and left.

Frank looked at the card, it read *'Powers Real Estate'*. He turned and started back to the barn, but noticed that Nancy had brought lunch and drinks out to the table he had found and fixed up near the porch. She waved at him to come and he stood there and smiled. A week or so earlier he had taken them all into Hatch and had bought the kids shoes, socks, and treated them to ice cream, then convinced Nancy to let him buy her a new dress, then he bought himself some new coveralls and shirts. He told her that he was not trying to get at her, but rather just helping her out, and she agreed, slightly.

He walked up to the table and saw the feast that was spread out, and gave a low whistle.

"There is chicken, potato salad, biscuits, tea, chips and water." She waved her hand, and cocked her head to one side.

"Not bad, where are the kids?" He looked deep into her eyes and saw a spark that he had never saw before.

"They are in the back playing on the hills." Her hair was curled up in a bun instead of straight, and she was wearing a light touch of lipstick and rouge on her cheeks. "They enjoy the steps you made up to the top."

He shrugged his shoulders and smiled, "The least I could do for them."

"The place looks absolutely great, I forgot how it really looked." She looked around, then suddenly the spark left her eyes and she dropped her head. "I guess after Roger died, I sorta gave up on the place."

"Was that your husband's name."

"Yes, little Roger is named after him." He looks a lot like him you know."

Frank nodded that he understood. She had three kids, the oldest was Robert, he would start school next year, and then came Roger, and then little Robin, each one about two to three years apart. He sat there looking at the barn and the corrals that he had started to build, thinking of what kind of animals he might be able to get to raise. She was partial to cattle, but the kids loved horses, maybe both.

"I noticed you down near the bridge, what are you doing to it?"

He came out of his thinking kind of groggily. "Huh" he looked at her and continued "Oh, I am reinforcing it and making it a little wider."

"Why are you doing that?" The glow started returning to her face.

"It is weak in certain places, and barely wide enough in others." He motioned toward the load of pipe he had brought in. "That should hold up real good after I'm done."

She nodded, she was also a little worried about where he was getting the money to do some of the things around here, but she bit her tongue and held back. Should she tell her brother, no that might ruin things. Her forehead was showing worry lines.

"I guess I should tell you," he pushed his plate away and wiped his mouth with a napkin. "Before I came here, I went to my father's funeral in Louisiana." He looked up as if trying to find the words. "He had a twenty-five thousand life insurance policy and I was the beneficiary." He paused and gave her a long look and continued, "So, if you are wondering, that is where I am getting the money." He had to stop and think about certain things he lied about, but others he told the truth.

She was shocked, and covered her mouth with her hand, "I-I-I didn't know, Jim never told me."

"I never told him." Frank was getting pretty good. But the one thing he did not lie about was his real name. *It was 'Frank Wilson Tanner', 'Frank Lee Morris' was from the bank hold up.* He got it them from the clerk and guard. He helped her pick up the dishes and trash and carry the things inside. Afterwards he left to go back and finish the door.

Frank preferred *Louis L''Amour books over Zane Grey* ones, so the last time he was in town, he purchased six of them. He marked the page then turned the light out to go to sleep, just then the door to the trailer open and then closed. He was laying there not knowing what to do or say. Then she slipped under the covers next to hi in the bed.

He gave her a quick look, she looked lovely in the moonlight, she reached up and put a finger over his lips, "Shhh, the kids are asleep."

He started to say something, but she said, "Just hold me, that's all, nothing else."

He laid there, one arm around her shoulders, the other under his head. He just about fell asleep himself when she got up and lightly kissed him then left. He laid there for a few more minutes then fell into a troubled sleep.

The next morning, there was no mention of the previous night. However, Nancy had a glow and move about her that he had never seen the whole time that he had been at the farm. She was humming a song, and even the kids were dancing about.

* * * SIX * * *

Frank was standing at the collection wall holding the glass that Josh had gotten at Alcatraz. He took a deep breath and turned around, he replaced the glass and said, "The rest you know. I married Nancy, purchased the land back that she sold and we had two more children."

He hobbled back to the desk and sat back down, looked at Josh over laced hands, "Well son, what do you think?" He had a questionable look on his face.

Josh stood up yawned and stretched, he was tired from sitting in the chair listening to his uncle's story. It was almost one, he walked over to the pot, poured the last cup of coffee and turned to look at his uncle. "That was the biggest cockamamie bullshit story I have ever heard." He took a drink then looking out the window said, "Do you give lessons to the drunks that we bring in?" He glared at his uncle.

"If you do not believe me, I left proof on your glass over there." He pulled out his pocket watch and looked at it. "I need to call Nancy, I told her I would be home at noon to do the will, and look, it is half past one."

Josh stood there staring blankly out the window, his thoughts racing at ninety miles an hour. Some of the things his uncle Frank Tanner had told him were true, but what about the rest, after all, this was the man who had raised him and his brother after his parents were killed in an auto accident. What should he do, what should he say, he did not know. He turned and looked at his uncle, "Tell you what Unc, you go home and let me think all this through, okay?"

His uncle looked at him with knowing eyes and said, "All right, you know where I live, I'll be waiting."

With that his uncle shuffled out of the office and the building and left in his truck. At that moment his wife came in, "what was that all about Josh?" She looked out the window, "I have never seen your uncle cry before."

"I just might be able to find out" he looked at her with knowing eyes. He placed the cup on the desk then started rummaging through it till he found the cards and envelope he was looking for. He sat and filled them out, they were for identification requests to the FBI with finger prints. He then retrieved the glass on the wall, and then painstakingly used his kit to dust it for fingerprints. He found some recent ones and some older ones, he carefully lifted them and placed them on the cards. When he was finished he washed the glass, put it back and prepared the envelope for mailing. He thought to himself, *'let's see what the FBI has to say'.*

The door to his office burst open and his wife Sara came rushing in, Josh was still there reminiscing over the photograph. "Josh, your aunt Nancy just called, your uncle had a heart attack, and the paramedics are on the way." She said short of breathe.

Josh stood up dropping the picture, it fell to the floor landing on a corner breaking and shattering the glass. He turned quickly to look at the wall, and the souvenir glass fell and broke as it hit the floor. He looked at his wife, "I'm on my way." With that he ran out of the office and drove at breakneck speed to his uncle's house.

He drove up to the front of the house, the paramedics had not arrived yet, and Nancy was sitting in a rocker on the front porch, her children consoling her. As he approached, she stood and pointed towards the back bedroom, he's back there, she looked up at him tears streaming down her face. He keeps asking for you over and over.

Josh nodded entered the house and started toward the back of the house. Frank had done a lot of changes to the house, he added two rooms and a bath above the original bedrooms. He had taken a wall out here and added one here, the overall effect made the house appear to be larger than it actually was. Josh entered the bedroom and saw his uncle lying there in the bed. He looked like he was drunk with hallowed eyes, his hair was a mess and needed combed. He approached the bed and knelt and noticed that he was breathing hard and his breathe was labored.

His uncle opened his eyes and saw his nephew and smiled, he motioned to him and Josh came a little closer. "In the bottom drawer of the nightstand is a shoe box I want you to have." He coughed and spittle ran down the sides of his mouth, Josh got a napkin and wiped it off.

He found the box and opened it, there on the bottom were some clippings of the prison break of Frank Morris and the Anglin brothers. Josh sifted through them looked at his uncle and his eyes started to tear up, "I believe you Unc." It was almost a whisper. His uncle motioned to him again and Josh leaned over so he could talk in his ear, he told Josh his finally wishes and how he wanted things to be after his death, Josh leaned back looked down at his uncle and said, "Do not worry Unc, I'll take care of everything." With that his uncle nodded closed his eyes, smiled a big smile, and died.

Josh walked back out onto the porch and his aunt, the tears streaming down his face, he looked at his aunt and she knew that her husband was gone, she rose and limped to him cursing her bad leg, she hugged him and said, "Let it all out Josh."

Josh and his brother were the last ones to approach the coffin and pay their finale respects, Josh took the envelope out of his coat pocket and put in the pocket of his uncle's coveralls. "I'll let you take this with you Unc, it will be our secret." Then his brother placed a single chrysanthemum in hands, and with that Josh closed and latched the coffin lid. He turned and looked at the congregation and nodded. Six deputies approached in dress uniform and black arm bands and carried the coffin out to the hearse. Josh watched and thought *'how ironic, the police giving Frank Morris a formal good-bye, if they only knew'*.

Six weeks later after obtaining permission from the National Parks, they were standing on the roof of Alcatraz Prison looking out toward San Francisco. Josh led the way sometimes carrying his aunt so that she could be there as well as Frank's children. He looked up and down the roof of the prison, the air shaft vent cover was still there lying on its side it was never returned to its proper place. It was as if it was left there to serve as a reminder to one of the many escapes from Alcatraz.

They finally made it to the north end of the building, which was over the old kitchen, Josh took off his hat and secured it with a tie string. He then lifted the urn with the ashes of his uncle in it. "Dust to dust, ashes to ashes, we commend to your keeping oh Lord, the mortal body and soul of 'Franklin Wilson Lee Morris Tanner' to your eternal keeping." The wind was strong and almost knocked Josh over, but he continued "He was a wonderful father, faithful husband and a valued friend and mentor, please let him find eternal rest and happiness."

With that he removed the lid and started spilling the ashes over the side of the building watching them swirl with the wind to the ground, out to sea and toward San Francisco. When it was empty Josh replaced the lid and handed it to his brother and helped his aunt up so that she could see where the ashes had gone. After a time of silence they turned to go back downstairs and the waiting boat that had brought them over from the mainland.

Josh looked up and at one of the ladders leading to the roof was FBI Special Agent Jack Dobsken. He was standing there with one leg on the railing, he looked over Josh, smiled, nodded, secured his hat, gave him a semi salute and then left.

* ABOUT THE AUTHOR *

Born Alvin George Busby of German-English-Indian parents, August 5, 1950 in Portales, New Mexico. His family later moved to Alamogordo, then to Tularosa and finally to Las Cruces, New Mexico where Alvin grew up in the Mesilla Valley. Later Mr. Busby Joined the Navy and spent twelve years in the service.

Mr. Busby has lived and worked in various cities and states doing various jobs from working on aircraft to computers. He developed an interest in writing while serving in the military, but gave it up because of the ridiculed he received from fellow shipmates. He rekindled his interest later when he literally ran into two of his favorite authors, James Clavell and Louis L'Amour while he was on vacation in southern California.

Mr. Busby has an unusual and remarkable writing ability, in that he sees stories. He can listen to a song, or hear a conversation and come up with a story to go along with it. Or he can watch a movie and come up with a totally new and different story from it.

Currently Mr. Busby is semi-retired and working part-time as a school bus driver. Mr. Busby has high hopes that his new found love for writing stories will work out so that he can fully retire and spend more quality and leisure time with his wife and grand-children.